I want to be
AN ACTOR

Ivan Bulloch & Diane James

STARRING

JASON

JORDAN

TOM

NICOLE

LIZZIE

CARLI

WORLD BOOK
In association with
TWO-CAN

Consultant Sue Barber
Photography © Fiona Pragoff
Illustrations Colin Mier
Additional Design Amanda McCourt

First published in the United States in 1996 by
World Book, Inc., 525 W. Monroe, 20th Floor, Chicago, IL USA 60661
in association with Two-Can Publishing Ltd.

Copyright © Two-Can Publishing Ltd., 1996

**For information on other World Book products,
call 1-800-255-1750, x 2238.**

ISBN: 0-7166-1742-0 (pbk.)
ISBN: 0-7166-1741-2 (hbk.)
LC: 96-60462

792

Printed in Hong Kong

1 2 3 4 5 6 7 8 9 10 99 98 97 96

CONTENTS

I WANT TO BE AN ACTOR

Putting on a play involves all kinds of different skills, and it's good to know as much as possible about all the different jobs involved. There are costumes to make, props and scenery to get ready, and makeup to apply. And, of course, there are all the acting techniques to learn, too! Acting may be hard work, but it's also fun and you'll make lots of friends.

Painting scenery and backdrops is just one of the jobs involved in putting on a play.

Dressing up will help you get into the character of the person you are playing.

This may look very strange, but it's a good exercise for loosening up your body and getting your imagination going.

Is he really going to blow the safe open? Or is he putting on a good show? As an actor your job is to be as convincing as possible!

A play needs an audience. Make sure as many people as possible know about it.

LETTING GO

Actors need to be as relaxed as possible. If they are tense, they may make mistakes. And they need to be healthy, too. Acting is a tough job!

aaahhh! ooohhhh! aarrggh!

Warming up

Before taking part in a play or rehearsing, actors do exercises to loosen up their bodies and voices. Breathing exercises are useful, too. Stand up straight and take slow, deep breaths. Feel your lungs fill with air.

Ooooh, aaaahhhh!

Try some voice exercises to help loosen up. Look in a mirror and make a yawning noise. Alter the shape of your mouth and use your lips and tongue. Practice singing, shouting, and whispering.

Use a mirror so you can see the shape of your mouth when you make different sounds.

Don't worry if you look silly; actors often have to do peculiar things!

6

I can nearly reach it! Just a little higher!

Giant cat stretch

Here's a great way to totally relax your body. Stand up straight with your head up and stomach tucked in. Stretch your arms up and reach as far as you can. Bring your arms and head down slowly, bending your back bit by bit. Keep going until you are curled up as tightly as you can. Now unfold very, very slowly until you are standing straight again.

Imagine you are reaching up to pick an apple from the tallest branch of a tree.

Now I'm as small as a mouse! Nobody can see me!

Keep your arms close to your head. Feel your body curling up bone by bone.

HAPPY OR SAD?

Now it's time to act!
Let's start with faces and
expressions. Watch the
people around you. Can you
tell from their faces what
they are thinking or feeling?

Happy

Showing how you feel
In real life, people don't think about
how they show their feelings.

Sad

When you're sad you may burst into
tears, and when someone tells a joke
you'll probably laugh. On stage you'll
have to switch feelings on and off, no
matter how you really feel.

Face up to it!
Your face is a very useful tool. You can
use your eyes, nose, and mouth to
show different emotions or feelings.

Puzzled

Try some of these in front of a mirror:
raise your eyebrows, wrinkle your
nose, open your mouth, make your
eyes into narrow slits.

People watch!
When you are out and about, look at the way people show their feelings. They may be angry, sad, impatient, or bored.

Angry

As soon as you get a chance, try imitating them in front of a mirror.

Scared.

Looking terrified is easy. I just have to think about snakes and spiders.

BODY LANGUAGE

Your face can tell a lot about how you feel, but so can the rest of your body. You can "say" a lot using only body language—without speaking at all. Actors use body language to be effective.

Walking tall

A confident, happy person will walk with her head up. She will not be afraid to meet your eye, and she might nod or raise a friendly hand. A shy person is more likely to walk with her head down and will avoid catching your eye.

If I've told you once, I've told you 5 million times!

I hope everyone is convinced by my acting!

How am I going to get out of this one?

Eyes wide open in fear, hand to mouth to cover up confusion

Chin out, shoulders up, finger pointed and shaking

Both people are making it very clear how they feel by their actions.

It's a lot more comfortable this way round!

This position suggests a relaxed, happy person.

Sitting pretty
Look at the way these people are sitting. What can you tell about them? Try the chair test and see how many different ways you can sit on a chair. What happens if you sit on the floor? Act out some different feelings while you are sitting.

These glasses make me look extremely stylish!

TIPS

★ Watch people when they are in groups—on the playground, at a football game, or waiting in line. How do they react to each other?
★ Watch television with the sound turned off. See if you can figure out what is going on.

Head up, shoulders back, and legs together. This boy looks anything but casual!

11

ACT IT OUT

Here are some great exercises to try with your friends. They will help get your imagination running wild and give you practice in working with space.

Worms have a funny effect on people. How would you pretend to take one out of a box?

What's in the box?
Sit in a circle with some friends and pass around an empty box. Take turns opening the box, and acting out what you imagine to be inside— no words allowed!

Acting without words is called miming. You'll probably find it quite difficult at first, but keep practicing and it will become easy. Use big, bold gestures with your hands and arms, and make your face work hard, too.

Walk About

When you are on a stage with other people, you will have to know where they are at all times. Learning to share a small space with others is very important. Practice this with some friends: walk around a room without bumping into anyone—look for the spaces and walk toward them.

That was a close one; I almost bumped into him!

Use this exercise to practice different ways of walking.

Pleased to feet you!

How do you do!

Now try walking around the room with your eyes focused on just one other person. Don't lose sight of him or her, but don't walk close to the person, either. And try not to bump into anyone else. Finally, walk around and greet each person you meet in a different way. Use a different voice, change the greeting, use new actions. Be as friendly or as unfriendly as you like!

QUICK CHANGE!

You are probably thinking about putting on a play by now. But before you start making costumes and gathering props, try some instant dressing up.

Be careful when you sit down!

Instant stuffing
Tie a pillow or cushion to your stomach. Now put on some oversize clothes. Presto! You're BIGGER!

Visit the kitchen and turn into a knight in shining armor!

Wooden-spoon sword

Colander helmet

Protect yourself with a saucepan-lid shield.

Paint hair and eyebrows on bag

Paint face with green face paint!

Monster madness
An ordinary brown paper bag can turn you into a scary Frankenstein monster in a matter of minutes.

Two in one

How many different characters can you turn yourself into with just one scarf or large square of fabric?

A pirate?

A bank robber?

it's kind of chilly up here above the clouds.

Up, up, and away!

Find the right hat, add a pair of swimming goggles, and you are an old-fashioned pilot!

Mmm! Those drinks look good!

I'd rather be a pilot!

An Arab in the desert?

Can I help?

Tie on an apron, fold a dish towel over your arm, and you have become a waiter. Add a tray and some glasses and look for thirsty customers!

PICK A THEME

You've exercised your voice and your body, and your imagination is running wild. Now put on an instant show!

Pick a theme

We chose the beach as the theme for our instant show. But there are plenty of other ideas. You could choose a windy day, a circus, or a camping expedition.

In the mood

Get together with your friends and talk about a day at the beach. What will the weather be like? What will you wear? What will you take with you? Will you have a good time? Try to smell the ocean and hear the waves!

Last time I made sand castles, they were leveled by a dog!

Leap high in the air to catch an imaginary beach ball.

Pretend to make a sand castle. Fill the bucket, turn it upside down, and lift it off carefully.

Making it up

When you are acting, make your gestures big and bold. You need to make sure that everyone in the audience can see what you are doing. Because you are not working with a script, you don't have to learn any words. You can make things up as you go along. This is called improvising. Dress up to help you get in the mood.

Owwww! It's got my big toe. Let go!

Imagine those nippy claws tightening around your toe!

She's not the only one feeling hot. I'd like ice cream, too!

My turn for a nip now!

LOOK THE PART

Now it's time to think about costumes. Dressing as the character you are going to play will help you look and feel the part.

New from old

Most costumes can be put together from existing clothes. Look for bargains in used-clothing stores and yard sales.

Keep a collection

Accessories, such as hats, belts, bags, scarves, ties, and jewelry are all useful. Keep your eye open for old glasses without lenses. Scraps of fabric, pieces of ribbon, and odd buttons may come in handy. It pays to be a hoarder, but try to keep your collection in some sort of order so that you can find things easily.

Stick cotton balls inside the rim of an old hat to make an instant wig.

I can't understand why everything looks upside down!

Necktie over shoulder adds to the disheveled look.

Look in magazines and newspapers for accessory ideas.

An old blazer is great for an absent-minded professor.

18

Let's get scary! Watch out birds, here I come!

Real scarecrows have a pole holding them up. You'll have to pretend!

Who's in charge?

If you are putting on a play with a large cast, it's a good idea to have someone in charge of the wardrobe. This person can help actors who need to change costumes quickly.

This oversize raincoat was a bargain from a used-clothing store.

Try your local pet shop for a supply of straw.

TIPS

★ Sketch out costumes on paper at an early stage. Then you can see immediately which things need to be made and which can be bought.
★ Keep the costumes for each character separate—large cardboard boxes may help.

You might have some things—such as overalls—in your closet.

TELL A STORY

Before you embark on a full-length play, try acting out some short scenes. You could use an existing plot or make up your own story line.

Larger than life

In a play the characters can behave in a totally off-the-wall way. They don't have to behave like normal people.

I only put my purse down for a second! I was sure it would be perfectly safe.

Whodunit?

We turned a simple burglary into something a bit more complicated!

I must remember that I'm the good guy now!

Fast-finger Freddy strikes again!

You don't need a lot of characters. In our play, the detective doubles as the bad guy.

Can't she see I'm just a fuzzy ball!

Rehearsing

As soon as all the actors have learned their parts, you can start running through individual scenes or the whole play. These practice runs are called rehearsals. The more complicated the play, the more time you'll need to rehearse.

Now she's spotted it. Notice the change in her expression and her arm movement.

Not much happening here, but she hasn't seen the spider yet!

Writing a script

When you have decided on a plot, you'll need to write the script. This means writing out the speeches, giving each character his or her own lines. You can also include some instructions for the actors. Give copies to all the players so that they can learn their lines by heart.

She's not hanging around to find out what happens next!

21

FACE CHANGE

It's amazing how you can change your character instantly with a little cleverly applied makeup. Here are a few hints and tips.

What you need

You can buy theatrical makeup in specialty shops, but we used ordinary makeup for the characters here. A selection of brushes—fat ones and thin ones—is useful!

Look for stick-on mustaches in costume shops.

Looking older

Start with a base coat of foundation. Choose a color fairly close to your skin tone and put it on with a sponge—not too thick! Add wrinkles with a soft eyebrow pencil.

Use an eyebrow pencil to draw on a curly mustache.

To find your natural wrinkles, frown or squint, and little lines will appear. Dust talcum powder on your hair and eyebrows to make them look gray.

Be bold

Stage makeup can be a lot stronger and more dramatic than normal makeup. To make your cheeks rosy, add several layers of blush over your base coat. Blend it in with your fingertips or a soft sponge.

Beauty spots can be added with a soft eyebrow pencil. Face paints come in bright, bold colors and are useful for special effects.

TIPS

★ Work in good, strong light, either near a window or under a lamp with a bright bulb.

★ Finish dressing as much as possible before putting on your make-up. This will help prevent smudging.

Remember the pillow trick? It will add a few pounds instantly.

Plenty of pink blush on cheeks and chin creates a healthy, cheerful look!

For a really glamorous look, try a curly blond wig, several coats of red lipstick, and lots of eye makeup.

How could anyone think I'm a criminal!

ODDS & ENDS

All the odds and ends that go into making a play look as real as possible are called props—short for properties.

Finding props
Some props may be simple household objects that can be borrowed. Others will be easy enough to make.

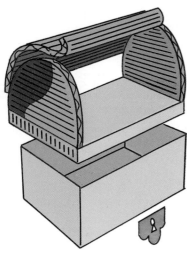

Paint plastic cups to make golden goblets. Use sequins and beads for jewels.

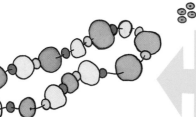

Use self-hardening clay to make a necklace. Or link paper clips together.

Draw a map on white paper, crumple it up, and soak it in a bowl of tea. When it dries, you'll have an ancient document.

Pirate's treasure
Use an old shoe box as the base for a treasure chest. To make the top, cut two rounded ends from cardboard and glue them to the lid of the shoe box. Cut a strip of thin cardboard to fit over the ends and glue or tape it in position. The illustration on the left may help. Cut out a paper lock and paint the box so that it looks like an old wooden chest.

A very royal throne

Start with a simple kitchen chair. Get a parent's permission first! To turn the chair into a throne, cut two sides and a back from thick corrugated cardboard. You can glue the baubles on afterward. Paint the pieces, adding shields and jewels. Tie the pieces to the chair.

I'm going to feel much more like a queen when I sit on this throne.

Measure the chair carefully before you cut out the throne.

I'd rather wear this than a collar!

Sticks of dynamite made from cardboard tubes tied together

Just call me King Rex!

Is it safe?

Find a sturdy cardboard box and paint it gray to look like metal. Paint some round boxes and glue them to the door of your safe to make a burglar-proof combination lock. Larger items, such as a safe or throne, are often called scenery because they help set the scene. On the next page, you'll find some more ideas.

SET THE SCENE

Organizing props and scenery for a play can take quite a while. Make a list of all the things you need right at the beginning of rehearsals.

Indoors or outdoors

Plays are often broken up into sections called acts. Each act may take place somewhere different, so you will need to change the scenery and props.

I'm going to paint a scene behind this window so it'll look like the real thing!

I'd better be careful when I sit on this!

The audience will not realize that this cleverly painted chair is actually flat!

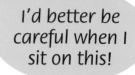

In order to make the changes as quickly as possible, it's a good idea to make scenery light and easy to move. Imagine how difficult it would be to move a heavy oak table and chairs in the few minutes you will have between acts!

26

Hide and seek

Here's a great way to make a boulder that doesn't weigh a ton. Cover a cardboard box with strips of double-sided tape. Peel off the backing strips and stick on balls of scrunched-up newspaper. When the box is covered, you can paint the paper in shades of gray.

Leave one side of the box open to make a cave.

Thornless cactus

Make a cactus like the one here and you definitely won't prick your finger. Cut two cactus shapes from cardboard. Make a slit from the bottom to the middle of one, and from the middle to the top of the other. Slot them together.

Better hurry up, it's almost time for the show...

When your boulder is finished, it will make a great hiding place!

GETTING READY

You've learned your lines, the costumes are made, and the props and scenery are almost ready. The big day is just around the corner!

Hope everyone can come!

Detective What exactly were you doing at 8:10 yesterday evening?

Tricky Well, it's hard to say exactly, but around seven I had my supper. That was fried chicken from the carry-out place on the corner. Then I went to see my friend Sam.

Detective Got you there, Tricky. Sorry to ruffle your feathers, but the fried chicken joint was closed yesterday.

Opening night nerves
Before you go onstage for your first show, have a final run-through of your lines. Do some stretching exercises to loosen up and some breathing exercises to help you relax.

Don't worry if you get butterflies in your stomach! It's perfectly normal, and they'll soon fly away.

Time and place
Make sure you have a big audience for your play. Send invitations to your friends in plenty of time and make some posters to promote the play. Don't forget to include the date, time, place, and name of the play.

I hope someone remembered to finish the pirate ship!

Almost there!
No matter how much you do in advance, there are bound to be last-minute panics! The backdrop may not be quite ready, or the star of the show may lose his or her voice. Make sure you have someone who knows the star's part and can stand in for him or her at short notice.

Before the final performance, have a run-through with costumes, makeup, and props. This is called a dress rehearsal.

I've had enough of this acting stuff!

PUTTING ON A SHOW

The big day has arrived, and it's time for the play to go on! Allow yourself plenty of time to put on your costume and makeup.

Can you hear me?
"Projecting" means being heard clearly without shouting. It's very important to project so that everyone will be able to hear every single word—even people sitting at the back.

IF YOU FORGET YOUR WORDS, DON'T PANIC! COVER YOUR MISTAKE AS WELL AS YOU CAN AND KEEP GOING AS THOUGH NOTHING HAPPENED.

★

NEVER EAT REAL FOOD OR DRINK ANYTHING ONSTAGE. IT COULD GO DOWN THE WRONG WAY.

HELP! HELP! That crocodile looks hungry!

Cardboard grass surrounded by blue paper gives the impression of an island.

Turn to page 24 to find out how to make a treasure chest.

Wait for it!
If you are putting on a funny play, wait for the laughter to die down before you continue.

INDEX

The show's over! Hope you enjoyed it as much as we did!